D1522195

Field Guide

Poems

Darío Jaramillo Agudelo

translated by
Don Share

MARICK PRESS

LIBRARY OF CONGRESS CATALOGUING
IN PUBLICATION DATA
Agudelo, Darío Jaramillo
Poems. Translations.
Field Guide/Darío Jaramillo Agudelo
ISBN: 978-1-934851-45-6

Copyright © 2012 by Marick Press

Design and typesetting by HSDesigns
Cover design by HSDesigns

Printed and bound in the United States.

Marick Press
P.O. Box 36253
Grosse Pointe Farms
Michigan 48236
www.marickpress.com

Distributed by spdbooks.org and Ingram

Portions of this work originally appeared in *AGNI, Salamander,* and *Poetry International.*

PREFACE

This "Field Guide," designed to be useful for the traveler, is conceived most of all for the pilgrim who chooses the initiate's road, who searches for cryptic, mystical signs; it is not so useful if merely read through from beginning to end. While one may read it in such a manner, the traveler will find it most helpful if he or she consults it as the need arises.

Contents

MORGUALOS

Morgualos love chimneys, white cotton shirts, the agapanthus, a tree called the seven-skin, the scent of fresh cilantro as it falls into soup, the sound of church bells, and days without clouds.

The Morgualos are makers of stills, three-cornered hats (but only for export), plows, watches, sextants, beakers, and candelabras.

They are printers, tailors, and cooks.

No one is more competent, diligent, well-organized, and skillful at his work than a Morgualo.

Morgualos accumulate things all through their lives: dried leaves from maple or walnut trees; beet-red flowers, or flowers colored like the Archibishop's red, pressed between the pages of a book; unobtrusive stones with strange shapes and textures; packing material for glass items; tiny filigrees of jade, silver, ivory, or wood; little trunks made of coconut or tin; small casks with subtle incrustations and decorations; laminas and poems; portraits and embroidery.

Morgualos place their charming fetishes in surprising places around their houses: a portrait might get stashed inside a dictionary; a brilliant red stone could end up in the refrigerator like a petrified vegetable; a poem could end up under a pillow; or a sketch on a bathroom wall. And whenever Morgualos stumble across these objects in their daily rounds, they smile.

There are three types of rain in the Morgualos' land: tepid splinters that fall in hot steam; a thick green rain—highly recommended for reviving marriages, or for intractable migraines; and, finally, a rain of pure water, so translucent that it can't be seen in mirrors, and which all Morgualos love.

The Morgualos' tools are: burins for grinding just the right shapes in their works; furnaces and tongs for smelting and picking up metal; forges and hammers, and Anvils—a word always capitalized, and seldom spoken aloud.

You won't hear a Morgualo mention Anvils; but it is known that Morgualos are in some kind of mental communication with them— they address prayers and supplications to them every time they must use an Anvil, and perform certain rituals when they are done using one.

Morgualos know riddles, and origami; they are master mechanics; they are expert in the use of chisels, trowels, and levels; they make shoe-makers' tools just as well as they make fine watches; in medicine, they know how to make use of prayers and roots—fibers and words are very useful to them, as are trances, and liturgical and thaumaturgical formulas.

Morgualos amuse themselves polishing stones; putting ceramics into the kiln and pies into the oven; by dancing the rigadoon; and by playing word-games.

A Morgualo year is measured by the number of appearances made by the phoenix. Each time one of these birds rises from a handful of ashes, another Morgualo year has passed by.

When a Morgualo dies, he is transformed into a useful object: a spoon, a fish-hook, tweezers, a bottle, a pair of eyeglasses, a chair, a shirt, a fan.

If a Morgualo falls in love, he does not need to tell the one he loves. All he has to do is dream of her three nights in a row, and she will know it.

Afterwards, the couple will be happy together, until the first moment of disaffection falls upon them, because a Morgualo is never afflicted with a love that is not reciprocated.

There are Morgualos who make invisible birdcages, and Morgualos who can't make them.

This is the only thing that divides the Morgualos, yet it does not constitute a motive for conflict or envy among them. Instead, Morgualos who can't make invisible birdcages admire those who can. At the same time, the latter, who comprehend that theirs is an innate ability, dependent upon unknown causes, are grateful for the signs of affectionate admiration shown them by the others, and customarily give them invisible birdcages as presents.

When a Morgualo has finished building an invisible birdcage, he has to open a window. A pair of tiny birds will fly in. The male is yellow and the female either red or blue, depending on the season. These are the invisible birdcage-birds who make that fatal flight through the window on the day a birdcage is finished.

An invisible birdcage becomes perceptible to the eye under the light of the moon. If it is a crescent moon, the delicate bars that form the cage look blue. If it is a waning moon, the cage appears to be made of a metallic liquid material, a kind of flowing mercury, and it turns silver until it dissolves in translucent, glassy whiteness while the moon becomes a sliver, a fine luminous banana.

Under the rays of a full moon, the invisible birdcage is golden, resplendent. It seems then to be made with threads of an amazingly pure light, through which the birds sing their most beautiful melodies.

FRUSOS

To be great players of Chinese checkers, to fly in a glider, to have their noses always in flowers, to drive arrows straight through bulls-eyes (and to be just as sharp with the fencing foil, and the bullet, and the word) . . . such are the strange dreams of Frusos.

Their nightmares: wrinkles in pants, socks strewn all over the floor, cigarette butts in ashtrays, deadly creases in bed sheets, even the hint of a mess, and the slightest asymmetry.

Frusos are punctual, courteous, precise. They spend much of their time hoping that they will keep their appointments.

The Fruso is a bit simple-minded, yet he knows how to sing 16th-century English motets, and is good at choral music and marches, not to mention rowing.

A Fruso's love lasts eight days, and is the only eternal love known to exist, because a Fruso's life also lasts eight days.

Few members of other species can appreciate the odd love life of the Fruso, which seems not only unusual, but downright grotesque. Yet it is conceivable—or is it?—that to Frusos, the sweet lie, "I'll love you forever," rings true. Among Frusos, love inevitably exists only between two, and not among three or more, which is common among us, or within one alone, as is more prevalent these days.

Each Fruso is born simultaneously with another. Their symmetry and complementarity are therefore genetically determined. Two Frusos destined to become a couple are placed in the same cradle for those few hours that make up their infancy. They are never apart from each other until death, which comes a week later—or even earlier, should a fatal crease in their bed sheets arise, a mishap that would cause painful convulsions that, wrecking their carefully made-up bed, would result in instant death.

Frusos live one for the other every moment of their lives, right up to the instant death unites them in Fruso Paradise, where the two are fused into a single being which, like every other lonely creature, passes its paradisal eternity searching for love.

SASICOS

The Sasicos, despite their many rulebooks, are very practical, and have a Department of Useless Rules; and the rules are carefully revised so that they don't become obsolete. Actually, there is little to do in this department, since Sasicos are so efficient. Sasicos have such good rules for uncorking wine, for example, that no Sasico has ever dropped the cork into a bottle. And if one ever did, he would be the laughing stock of his neighborhood, and the shame of his family.

Sasicos also have obligatory rules of civility. Any Sasico who raises his voice is automatically turned into a toad. So is any Sasico who walks on the grass. And there are always some foreigners who—inadvertently, but rudely—cut into the front of a Sasico line, and they, too, are turned into toads.

Punishment is always automatic, thanks to a retaliation gas mixed into the atmosphere of Sasico lands and oceans.

The Sasico Queen wears a red tunic, fringed with fluffy white fur. The cape seems very heavy, and is long enough to reach her feet. She also wears a gold crown with white incrustations shaped like the sun.

The Queen doesn't have the power to punish anyone; the punishment gas takes care of that. But of all Sasicos, she is the only one who can turn toads into blue princes.

Consequently, whenever robust and elegant blue princes are needed to work in mines or jackhammer streets, the Sasico Queen kisses as many toads as necessary.

If a Sasico wants a rose, the Manual of Desire is consulted: Book of Plants, Flower Chapter, Rose Section. The manual tells precisely when and where a rose may be encountered, as well as how to care for one; it also contains advice about the cuts and pricks caused by roses.

TINGUANOS

Tinguanos can fly after lunch. They only have to close their mouths and relax their eyelids, and they can fly for an hour—maybe two, if their gramophones are working.

The rest of the day, Tingaunos have to sit up in their little windows answering questions from other Tinguanos, or, if they are lucky, they may spend the day waiting in line to do something for a Tinguano who is sitting in a little window.

If a Tinguano wants a rose, all he has to do is snap his fingers, and he will have one—provided roses are in bloom, because other seasons of the year, finger-snapping retrieves various kinds of fruits and vegetables.

If a Tinguano wants a rose, snaps his fingers, and obtains, say, a carrot, or jasmine, or an apricot instead, the best he can do is ask a Tinguano in a little window how to get a rose.

ICNIDOS

Icnidos experience emotions depending upon the expressions on their faces. As a result, Icnido education is an apprenticeship in face-making: the appearance of joy—which instantly causes that feeling of exaltation and expressive pleasure which every species recognizes; the appearance of restfulness, deep sleep, and slack-mouthed, dumbfounded dreaming; all the expressions of happiness or ecstasy.

It is not the case that, as for many species, passion is reflected involuntarily in the face. On the contrary, expressions are chosen strictly through the intellect; facial appearance is like a filter for one's disposition, and is anterior to passion. And once—through a rictus smile, or a studied movement of the eyes—some feeling, disposition, or passion appears on an Icnido's face, the consequences are inevitable. An Icnido can, for instance, obtain an orgasm simply by making the face of someone having an orgasm.

In spite of this ability to choose any passion, physical sensation, disposition, etc., freely and intellectually, there are certain expressions that are forbidden, and some that are even kept secret. These are in the exclusive domain of a caste of initiates, a caste nearly extinct at present. These Icnidos forbear the appearance, and this is understood among them, of vengeance and greed.

No one communicates with elephants more effectively than Icnidos. It's not even a question of ability, but of a kind of interpenetration one might be tempted to call love. But it isn't love. Naturally, such a symbiosis arouses affection and deep feeling between the elephants and Icnidos, but this isn't exactly love. When an elephant communicates with an Icnido, he wiggles his ears in a certain way, he blinks slowly. He smiles.

We don't know if the relationship between elephants and Icnidos is characterized more by similarity or contrast. It wouldn't do us any good to understand how they communicate, since it wouldn't tell us anything new about elephants.

We do know that the fragrance of jasmines poisons the Icnido atmosphere and causes genetic deformities. Deformed creatures are born whose faces are masked with irreversible expressions. There is one particular Icnido who permanently bears the astonished look of a child at the circus, and who therefore—as would be the case with any Icnido—goes through life imprisoned in continual amazement, astounded at everything in his life, as predetermined by a face which registers incredulity with each sensation: an Icnido who discovers in each moment the miracle, or inexpressibility, of being alive and knowing it.

Because of such jasmine-induced genetic damage, there are Icnidos born with expressions that produce the most grotesque passions, such as zoophilia, or sheer pain. There have been cases of Icnidos born with puckered-up frowns, the telltale sign that they are destined to become judges. There is a law that permits euthanasia for Icnidos born with the appearance of having an earache, since no one can imagine how long and hard an earache would be for an Icnido born looking like he had an earache.

Essential skills for any Icnido: learning how to make certain faces, and remembering all the right facial expressions.

If an Icnido wants a rose, this indicates that earlier on he must have made the face of someone wanting a rose, and we may presume that such an Icnido knew how to look like someone who wants roses. With this very look on his face, he can go to the florist, where the girl behind the counter will understand him immediately.

Among Icnidos there are morning-days and evening-days. A day never comes for Icnidos which has both the yolk of the morning and the white of the evening.

Perhaps a day might begin softly with a slow morning, flooded with the light of an early sun, followed by a weakening midday that lasts six hours, until the moment of total darkness suddenly arrives.

Then again, some days there is an unseasonable leap from the darkness of dawn right to midday, and the hours of light pass through a lethargic afternoon that congeals into a half-light lasting for hours, as if dusk had rested a long time before unleashing its final torrent of darkness upon the Icnidos.

DEMITONES

Four characteristics distinguish the Demitones: their changing colors, their dealings in gold, the manner in which they reproduce themselves, and their photographic memories.

None of these characteristics helps us to understand these others: a mania for attempting the impossible, a bad habit of using foul language in every bit of conversation, a penchant for dancing in the street, and skill at typing.

The Demitones change color every two years. Beginning with the fifth change, they can choose any color they wish, and on their birthdays, they will automatically turn that color. If a Demitone stays the same color on his birthday, then this will be his death-color.

Death, for a Demitone, can be quite peaceful, if he is white, and somewhat less so if he is green, the dull, clear color of lemon juice. But there is nothing more painful than a Demitone's red death: it begins with a convulsion that goes on for six weeks; on the final Wednesday, the convulsions erupt in a muffled explosion, which is not repeated— and then the Demitone dissolves in a blackish-red mist which feeds the birds of the land.

Why, knowing that their deaths will be so terrifying should the color red overtake them, do Demitones prefer red over all other colors?

Because if they turn red, they can receive a kind of beatific vision when they fly kites, play billiards, or plant roses of that special color.

Demitones have no eyelids: they go through life with open eyes, memorizing everything they see in cinematic detail, even though they might not really be looking. In fact, Demitones have an organ that permits them to project any visual image they may recall onto a screen no matter how long ago they saw it.

Leaving aside the matter of their typing (how can they help but be good at it, given that they have so many fingers, and that their typewriters have so many keys?), no one seems to know where Demitones get their gold, their inexhaustible supply of gold. No one sells it to them, and there aren't any alluvial mines or veins of ore in their country, nor are there any remnants of reserves of precious metals. What is known is that the Demitones pay for all their purchases from foreigners with nuggets of gold.

Gold clearly doesn't matter to the Demitones (if they were to value it, they would be able to make fabulous profits in its international trade); and they affect to judge what they remember—in other words, anything they have seen—with neither disgust nor pleasure.

The most unusual thing about this species is the preamble to their existence, their gestation. It is known that Demitone sexual reproduction requires three individuals. Here's how things happen: three amorous Demitones lock themselves up in a copulation chamber, a dark enclosure that protects the modesty of these eyelid-less creatures. Inside, they make love with their characteristic sensuality, and when the door is opened after two weeks of intense but very subtle eroticism, *four* Demitones emerge: in addition to the parents (each one the color they chose on their last birthdays) there will be a brand-new, invisible, translucent Demitone.

No one can see or hear a newborn Demitone. But he, able to observe things with his lidless but retentive eyes, will see whatever he pleases.

A newborn Demitone can choose or refuse his existence. After two years of invisibly observing and preparing for life, the young and imperceptible Demitone freely decides whether to fade away into nothing or achieve real existence and become a white Demitone, white invariably being the color he will be in his first change.

ARFOS

If an Arfo plays any stringed instrument, his body will rapidly grow covered with sores.

This is the Arfo's curse, the scourge of the species: Arfos have forests thick with the finest wood for making guitars and violins. Arfos have the best workshops for making stringed instruments, and they are the best artisans in the trade. In fact, their entire economy is based on the production of violins.

But they are simply unable to play them, because the musical plague would take over their bodies.

For Arfos, words change meaning daily. For others, this would be a problem threatening survival itself, but since Arfos have absolutely nothing to say to each other, they're not aware of any problem.

At any rate, the cultivation and treatment of the wood, cutting and planting of trees, and all the secrets of instrument making are known instinctively, so there is no need for communication.

Arfos drink a viscous black liquor which makes anybody who drinks it, except for Arfos, go mad. With rudimentary stills—and a magic formula—Arfos distill the darkest parts of certain nights, and under the intense light of the newly shadowless moon—since all the shadows are now potable—they get drunk on dense darkness made into liquor.

If an Arfo wants a rose, he will never know for certain that he really wants one, since the word, *rose*, like every other word, changes meaning every day.

If an Arfo wants a rose, one day he might think roses are sharp instruments used for moving earth, and another day he will believe that he is dealing with *carne asada con salsa*, and only by accident, one day, an Arfo may come to believe that the sense of the word has to do with a certain plant, that the word means thorns on a stem, and colored petals.

ETUCARBOS

Etucarbos are convinced that the young are wretched, and that one pays for fulgency with a tormented soul. The fanaticism, the fondness of the young for messianic ideas, theories, and dogmas, limits them and blinds them; such is the Etucarbo assessment of their young. And, they add sententiously, this wretchedness stems from the fact that the young concoct ideas that are free flowing, but too rough.

Because of all this, Etucarbos are born after 40 years of gestation.

Etucarbos are made of vapor and tears, though it seems they have a skeletal structure which allows them to die standing up, and, before that happens, to sit up all night.

Just as their gestation lasts many years, their physiological make-up is quite complicated, especially concerning the intricate chemistry of their production of tears.

The list of things that can kill Etucarbos is endless—stumbling across a hummingbird's corpse, leaving identification papers at home, looking at a beaver's eyes, wearing a ruby-red sweater, insinuating scorn . . .

Etucarbos are good at setting off explosions, and cracking military ciphers. It was an Etucarbo who gave us fine translations of dogs' language, and an Etucarbo who invented the alcohol-pillow.

If an Etucarbo falls ill, he is liable to explode at any moment, endangering the lives of other Etucarbos. For this reason, all sick Etucarbos are put to death.

No one is more afraid of exploding than an Etucarbo. Etucarbos also dread favorable horoscopes, and being left without dessert. They abhor birds, and tomato soup.

An Etucarbo never loses his composure, or his keys; he never interrupts or listens; nor does he miss any opportunity to bring up the unhappiness of the young.

Etucarbos are never happy.

They are afflicted with bursts of energy. They'll straighten up the house, take a bath, groom themselves, sweep the street, check on the sowing of their fields (taking care never to step on a hummingbird's corpse, or look into a beaver's eyes), do the weeding, milk the cows and goats, and make tools.

In these fits of activity they catch up on put-off chores, thanks to a special capability for prioritizing actions and bringing them speedily to completion, so that nothing will be left unfinished when an attack of lethargy comes.

When indolence seizes them (which is analogous to its opposite condition, work-fever), the Etucarbos are incapable of finishing any task, except that of taking whatever steps are necessary to get quickly into bed.

During these bouts of apathy, Etucarbos close the curtains, bury themselves under the covers, and whine about the young—but only with submissive sighs and whimpering, not with any puffery or derision, and scarcely any cursing, or anything at all forceful. They weep a little, and then they get tired.

When they get work-fever again, they toss and turn in bed: first they try one side, then the other, face up, then face down—they can't get comfortable; then, after trying out every conceivable position, they toss and turn some more, turning themselves inside out like a glove: what was outside ends up inside, and vice versa. So, looking inside themselves, stretched out in bed, full of apathy, ennui, and laziness, as if they'd been given an anesthetic, they outline each phase of the work that lies ahead. Then, turning themselves inside out again like a glove, they get up and go to work.

If an Etucarbo wants a rose, he just wants it to see it wither.

HERCOS

Hercos cultivate flies and spiders; they have nurseries for asps and hornets. In Herco cities, one hears an endless buzzing, something that echoes through the air, an atmospheric resonance: it is the sound of their flies fluttering, their creepie-crawlies and their bugs whizzing through the air, stirring it up.

The Hercos move without movement—they're whisked along rippling currents of air. They eat beetles.

Their movements are involuntary, and depend upon capricious oscillations of flat slabs in the ground that suddenly shift one way, and then the other, without a single Herco being able to explain just how this comes about. The truth is, Hercos are uninterested in finding explanations for anything; it doesn't even occur to them that such things as explanations exist.

Why would a Herco want roses? He wouldn't. In fact, no rose exists in the Herco universe, just as television didn't exist for the Chaldeans. No plant exists for the Hercos, nor is there a word "petal" or a word "rose."

If a Herco wants a rose, neither he nor any other Herco knows what it is he really wants. A *what*?

If a Herco wants a rose, at most he would be wishing for some kind of gibberish.

If a Herco wants a rose, it's because he is completely crazy.

BROTAUROS

They hear the drumbeat of the distant galloping which announces the invader.

In night thunder they divine the omen of the attackers' gunfire.

They hold frequent war dances to talk to their god, who is simultaneously a bull, a tree, and a stone that gushes water. They prepare for these dances with an inebriating potion that puts them in touch with the land of some fish that fly and vomit fire; there, they can speak with Bull-Tree-Fountain.

When not preparing their intoxicants, Brotauros are busy with cleaning their weapons, or target-practice. They never go hunting, though, since they are vegetarians.

Brotauros come in two sexes. The first is born with a weapon in its hand, and the second with a sewing needle, a sickle, and a case of phosphorous.

Nevertheless, one shouldn't suppose that the tasks performed by the second sex indicate that they are not as obsessed with warfare as the first sex. On the contrary, they execute their work as if they were always on the eve of a great siege; they maintain reserves of food, clothes and fuel as if they were facing a great enemy army, taking for granted that Brotauros of the opposite sex have sufficient fighting skills to resist.

Though there are two sexes, Brotauros do not reproduce through any kind of physical contact; they do it through laughter. If a Brotauro bursts out laughing, and another Brotauro is infected by the outburst, then right at the spot where their waves of laughter collide a brand-new Brotauro will appear, already equipped with the instruments of war, or with the means of producing fire, food, and articles of clothing.

There is no point denying it: Brotauros do not understand how useful binoculars are. Nor would such a thing interest them—their passion for lenses goes far deeper. It would never occur to them to consider lenses as instruments. The aesthetic value of lenses is so great that Brotauros conserve them—even exhibit them—in privileged places in their homes, so that they can admire them with *oohs* and *ahs* of pleasure, without touching them, circling round and round to appreciate their loveliness in full.

Once, a Brotauro who was rather more curious than the others took a pair of binoculars and tried to figure out what it was used for. After several hours of experimenting, it occurred to him to put the binoculars up to his eyes and look through the lenses while standing near a window. But the night was so dark that he couldn't see a thing.

Brotauros don't distinguish between love and death. Death, as such, does not exist for Brotauros, although they do disappear. They disappear, just as the fruits of love disappear.

It happens this way: When young, Brotauro families arrange marriages for their children. Sometimes, when Brotauros of one sex or the other decrease in number, only the richest of the abundant sex succeed in obtaining a spouse. The sewing-needle-sexed spouse devotes herself to raising her offspring, cultivating a vegetable garden, cooking, making clothes and washing them, and an endless number of other domestic chores. The weapon-sexed Brotauro is faced with far more serious tasks, ones that are transcendent and epoch-making, like preparing for war by making weapons and performing rough training exercises.

In spite of their preparedness for war, Brotauros have never had the opportunity to put their skills to the test, because they have never yet had a war. This means that they have no war heroes, and there is some question about how to motivate the troops; but armed struggle may be excluded as a cause of Brotauro mortality.

When the family is grown, after many years spent under the same roof, sleeping in the same beds, and drinking the same milk, suddenly one night, when the three moons of their world are shining brightly, a

Brotauro couple will begin desperately making love. Older Brotauros eventually discover the pleasures that the body of one affords another. Remember that they reproduce though the coincidence of laughter, which means that the carnal instinct is not tied to reproduction. So physical desire arrives late in life for them, with such intensity that there comes a moment in which two naked Brotauros can't help but be joined together.

When this happens, they fuse together, little by little, until they become a single luminous Brotauro, one that rapidly fades away in a light that leaves behind a tiny seed as its only trace.

If a Brotauro wants a rose, he sows one of these love-seeds, and in a few days he has his rose.

CHISGAROS

A Chisgaro's eye functions effectively over great distances. But closer up, a Chisgaro sees less. At two meters, the Chisgaro is blind. His arms wave around without ever emerging from the darkness, though the length of his legs allows him to see vaguely where he is going.

Chisgaros place mirrors far from their bodies, since they can only see themselves at a distance. And when they make love, Chisgaros don't see each other at all.

Knowing that Chisgaros lack a sense of smell, it is easy to guess that if a Chisgaro wants a rose, it would just be to feel it.

GUZGUCES

If a Guzguce wants a rose, he will have to think it through, step by step. The length of the stem. The tip of each thorn. The shape and color of each petal. He will have to think about its scent, and conceive of the tender sensation of touching it, so that he will believe himself to be cherishing this illusion.

If a Guzguce wants a rose, he has to know his rose completely, and have it fixed in his memory. Then the rose will grow out of his head, and the happy Guzguce can cut it, and, jumping with joy, deliver it as a present to his beloved.

BLOMORFOS

Everything in a Blomorfo's life comes about this way: First, an object is drawn, down to the smallest details, then the secret magic formula that each Blomorfo just barely whispers is said, and then the real McCoy springs into existence from the plan, the idea preceding the reality. Obviously, Blomorfos use up lots of paper and pencils, but they just have to draw the shape of a new ream, trace the outline of the pencil they want, say the spell, and they'll have at their disposal the necessary materials for making food and clothing, a house and some furniture, and, what's more, a few children.

Blomorfos reproduce the same way they create reality: by drawing. A Blomorfo draws another Blomorfo, recites the formula, and that Blomorfo will be his child, even if the Blomorfo who's doing the drawing is old.

Blomorfos die because a drawing can be erased by time, or because someone carelessly smears it with marmalade, or tears the sheet on which the unlucky Blomorfo was traced.

A Blomorfo's life is spent sitting at tables and desks. If a Blomorfo wants a rose, he will have to draw the rose in exacting detail so that it can enter reality. As he traces out the rose, it springs into existence: a singular, transparent rose.

MILACOS

Milacos have brilliant feathers on their wings and spines. Their Mondays are white and their Saturdays yellow, but all the other days are translucent and can't be seen, even under lamplight.

On invisible days, Milacos doubt their own existences and wait anxiously for a Monday or Saturday to make sure that they haven't disappeared. If it should be a Milaco's fate to yawn on a Wednesday, he will feel more sure of himself, more certain that he is not merely the victim of his own delusions.

Milacos master the Sanskrit language, but never speak it—possibly because they know no one with whom they can communicate in it. They do not speak it among themselves since were they to do so, the resultant nostalgia would give them leprosy, a feverish insomnia, or the obsession to play a radio full-blast until it produces in them a kind of frenzy which explodes into tremendous madness.

DINECOS

Dinecos play the cowbell well; everyone knows that a decent orchestra should have a Dineco on the cowbell. They are also good at making congas, flutes, and viola da gambas, particularly on melancholy days, or days on which left-handers are born.

A Dineco born left-handed can play dominos well, but can't masturbate; the latter isn't so important because Dinecos never masturbate, since they only feel amorous once every three years, on a pre-set date, accompanied by their three partners.

An illustration of Dineco love and affection is the way they threaten to eat their children alive: they move right up close, their four powerful hands raised, open up their enormous mouths, baring their canines in a demonstration of ferocity common to all carnivorous species, and bellow into their children's faces from the intimate distance of a kiss, or of a first bite.

They need only hear the sound of horses' hooves to forget whatever preoccupies them. Dinecos have a tendency to become preoccupied and waste their time ruminating. Their days are spent between doubt and sadness, until they happen to hear a horse's hooves—then the things they imagine deep down disappear. At that moment, a euphoria takes over which—though all-encompassing—manifests itself with little ado if the horse is trotting, but which produces a fit of loud enthusiasm, and a crazed, possessed kind of dancing, if the horse is heard to gallop. There's no need even to mention the kind of ecstasy which results from *seeing* a horse, or, what's more, actually stroking a horse's mane. And there's no joy greater than that experienced in parts of a Dineco town through which an unexpected cavalcade bursts.

KODAS

If a Koda wants a rose, he won't want it to get another Koda to go to bed with him.

A Koda would never succeed in getting a rose for such a purpose. He would tell the Koda he's seducing that he would *like* to have a rose to give her, and then she would be ready to be his, and remain seduced as if struck by lightning.

At that point, the first Koda doesn't need a rose for anything.

Every single night, seven stars fall into the craters of each volcano in the Koda region. The Kodas bet on which volcano will land the first star, and then they bet on which volcano will be the last to fill with stars. Still, Kodas are afraid of this natural spectacle, and prefer to vanish when it occurs.

PERINTIDOS

Perintidos are tense and highly spiced. When two Perintidos fall in love, they must eat onions together, and eat nothing but onions. If there are three, though, the diet shifts to cauliflower.

Perintido lovers stick their tongues out, and nibble, slobber and suck, and eventually succeed in slurping down their partners. When this happens, the swallower must walk very softly and suffer insomnia till he vomits up the Perintido he swallowed. On that day, he will give the other a suitcase.

It has not been determined which food causes four Perintidos to fall in love, but it is known that sniffing a certain secret root can lead to the marriage of five Perintidos.

If a Perintido wants a rose, this Perintido is in love with another Perintido. If a Perintido wants two roses, then he loves two Perintidos. When he gets his rose or roses, it will be because he had enough money left over after buying all those onions or cauliflower.

When there's a harvest, say, of onions, there will be many couples. Yet why, if they eat the same things, don't some of the couples fall in love with the others, and why don't all Perintidos eventually fall in love with each other?

This, in fact, happens on one special day of each year. All the other days, a couple sets a special time, producing a unique rhythm for their onion eating. So some couples do, with difficulty, crossbreed with others.

What happens when a Perintido couple runs out of onions, or a trio runs out of cauliflower, or a quintet runs out of tuber-roots?

Their claws become sharp, gross, and firm, their lips turn into tough, pointy beaks, their feverish caresses become mortal attacks, and their kisses leave deep wounds. They die, their blood sprinkling the earth.

From this shower of blood a new Perintido sprouts who will dedicate his infancy and early youth to learning how to grow onions, cauliflower, and roses.

PELICHAROS

Time comes to Pelicharos in tiny bottles, though no Pelicharo knows where these bottles come from; each bottle contains one month.

There are Pelicharos who, when they are having problems, take two bottles of time (any more than that would be a lethal dose), fall asleep, and wake up two months later, when everything has passed. On the other hand, if they are content, they drink down their bottles very slowly, and there will be plenty of time for them to feel calm, even paralyzed, in a fit of happiness, a spasm of felicity that takes them altogether beyond time.

Pelicharos are tender, gentle, friendly. No one is more accommodating than a Pelicharo. No Pelicharo is disagreeable; if one were to be so, he would simply not be a Pelicharo.

Pelicharos know in advance what a visitor wants, and anticipate the latter's articulation of it by offering the desired object with the wonderful, expansive, innocent, childlike smile so characteristic of Pelicharos.

Guests are treated this way until they feel relaxed enough to start ordering around their hosts, who run to bring chairs, serve tea, install iron window gratings, and come up with the most ordinary and the most extraordinary things. Then the Pelicharos mince their visitors into little pieces and swallow them down, shred by shred.

IZOPIROS

Izopiros love nothing more than money. They have great forests that they turn to pulp, just to have the paper for printing money. They own enormous printing plants that run during the 27 hours of their day, and the four hours of their night, printing millions upon millions of dollar bills.

They love nothing more than money, and own immense mines from which they can extract the metals necessary for the alloys in their jingling coins, which are like little mineral stars.

Izopiros love money so much that they eat money. Their houses are made of layers and layers of coins—which can be eaten in times of extreme hunger. All of an Izopiro's needs amount to money, which they accumulate, and which they love more than anything.

They fall in love each Wednesday. On Wednesdays, they puff up and become very large. They swell and swell, in proportion to how much in love they may be. Then a moment comes when they are physically unable to grow more inflated—and they explode. In the wee hours of Thursday, when their love is all spent, they return to the endless task of making and consuming money.

If an Izopiro wants a rose, it would be to engrave it on a bank note, to be a symbol of value, embossed in relief on the obverse of some extremely valuable coin.

BREGISLAOS

Bregislaos come out of the water to chat and to kill things that live in their oceans. But they pass almost all their day-nights in the darkest regions of their seas where no light ever penetrates, and where the weight of the water overhead flattens their bodies into rocks hard as diamonds.

There in the depth of the depths, the Bregislao is a tidy little stone that passes miraculously through the water's impenetrable density, and tries to get its large, useless navy to solve chess problems and devise puns.

If a Bregislao solves a chess problem, he floats up to the surface. If he makes up a pun that is so unusually witty that it is dangerous enough to smother someone with laughter, he bobs up to the surface. There are some Bregislaos who have never seen light.

When a Bregislao reaches land, his body grows manifestly larger. He becomes talkative and wants to tell the whole world his solution for some chess problem, or share a great pun.

It is best to pay attention to these Bregislaos, because if you don't, they will bother you until you are left permanently breathless.

On land, the sex of a Bregislao may be determined by his smell. There is a wide variety of odors expelled by Bregislaos, such is the diversity of their sexes.

The predominant Bregislao odors are those of flowers. There are Bregislaos redolent of jasmine, others of the agapanthus, and still others that radiate the sweet scent of violets; there are Bregislaos with scents characteristic of the most unusual plant species.

There are also other smells, which might be said to originate from the whale, or from some cave, from fire, or from a wound—thousands of scents.

The important thing is that when two Bregislaos have exactly the same odor—which is like saying that one would swear that the other doesn't smell—the physical attraction is immediate.

When the two perceive each other, and discover each other to be odorless, they get right up close to perform their quick sexual act. They immediately separate again, still in such ecstasy (they can prolong their orgasms indefinitely) that neither even bothers to let anybody know about the solution to a chess problem, or of a pun they may have made up.

UYERTINOS

Uyertinos are globes of light. At least, that is they way they look to anyone who is not an Uyertino. But they see each other distinctly, as dark, corporeal creatures. If two Uyertinos are talking near you, you won't be able to hear them, and you'll just see two globes of light. For this reason, Uyertinos can easily be mistaken for the headlights on a car.

But for them it's all very clear. Uyertinos with blue eyes are considered most fortunate, since other Uyertinos are obliged to satisfy their wishes without a word. If a blue-eyed Uyertino wants more makeup, or more mango sherbet (which are surely the first things one of them would ask for), any Uyertino who is nearby has to come up with the makeup or sherbet.

If it were up to them, Uyertinos would always wear makeup. And not just for vanity's sake. They actually derive nourishment from knowing that they are well presented. If they start looking sloppy, if they get a little mud on their boots, they start to languish, to waste away, and could vanish in a matter of minutes. Because of this, Uyertinos always take along a purse. That way, an emergency is quickly dealt with, and tragic things won't happen, like the Uyertino at the beach who became disheveled when a breeze blew, and died trying to reach a brush. Or the Uyertino trumpet-player whose lipstick got smeared and had already died by the time they found his makeup case.

If an Uyertino wanted a rose, several things could happen. If he had blue eyes, every Uyertino who heard him say so would have to scurry around looking for one, until an Uyertino was found who had one— and he'd have to give it up without a word, once it was explained that a blue-eyed Uyertino wanted it.

If the Uyertino wanting the rose had red eyes, or yellow, or white eyes, he would have to look for one all by himself. And if he found one, it would surely be taken from him in a flash, because there would always be some blue-eyed Uyertino around who'd want it.

YICARINOS

A Yicarino thinks he is five Yicarinos. If he wants a rose, he will think that he wants five roses. The only number Yicarinos know is the number five. Consequently, he is one, and yet five, and the god he worships is one, and yet also five. For Yicarinos, there is only the number five.

In the Yicarino language, there are no vowels because their speech sounds like a kind of grunting. Every Yicarino thinks he speaks five languages.

Apart from these singularities—or pluralities—of character, the Yicarinos are pleasant all week, except Sundays. And they are known for their skill with the harquebus, aviculture, the mazurka, ombre, cooking, and flashy dressing. No one is more elegant than a Yicarino. And Yicarinos carry little notebooks for recording their witticisms. They also carry calculators (which only help a little, given their confusion between five and all the other numbers), magnetic compasses, and microscopes.

On Sundays, they are physiologically designed to be reproachful and unpleasant, so you should be prepared not to say a word to them then. If you do, anyway, they will simply maintain a prudent silence. Yicarinos know that they will be vindicated later on; the unfortunate person who insists on bothering them on a Sunday will perish a few days later in a fortuitous, but fatal accident.

At bedtime, the Yicarino puts his hand into his mouth and draws out all his bones. He neatly deposits them in a chest, takes inventory of them, and lays out his visible part on a blanket, because his invisible part scares away anybody who might be around.

Ghostly whistling, laughter, murmuring, more whistling, flashing lights, far-off screaming, howling, squalling, storming, thunderbolts and lightning flashes—the invisible part of a Yicarino has these things at its disposal to frighten away even the most unflappable traveler who passes through Yicarino territory.

HUPILAS

Every single day, as if ordained by the hand of fate, Hupilas lose one thing, and find another.

Security guards are worthless, precautionary measures, inventories, vaults, duplicates, alarms—all worthless. Every single day they lose one thing, and find another.

Opening the refrigerator, a Hupila might suddenly find a bejewelled crown that another lost. And then again he might be searching for, say, his left shoe, and find that it has vanished forever.

Even so, Hupilas know how aleatory each possession is; their nature leads them, irrepressibly, instinctively, to cherish seven fetishes over the course of their lives. They have a list from the time they are very little. For example: a red undershirt, a fountain pen, some eyeglasses, a glass sculpture, a leather wallet, a silver coin, a dictionary. The list might include things that they don't even have yet, but which will be theirs at some point, and of which they will become covetously, passionately fond.

On losing his first object, the Hupila will feel torn up inside, a distinct new sensation. And so the loss of each of the seven fetishes will be like a change of skin for the Hupila until the seventh object disappears, and then, bereft of any more feelings, he will die for lack of interest in life.

The bicycle is part of Hupila religious ceremonies. It has to do with a recent, but widespread cult among them. One day not long ago, a Hupila was visiting the land of bicycles, and was quickly charmed by the bicycle's beauty, grace, and usefulness; he spread the word to others. Now on holidays the main ritual consists of donning a cycling outfit and mounting a bicycle.

If a Hupila wants a rose, it would be to replace one he lost the day before.

RISPIDOS

If anyone knows a Rispido, or has any dealings with one, the first thing he will say is that he has been in contact with the very model of sanity. The testimony is universal: no one is wiser, more tactful, or more prudent than a Rispido. There is no one more respectful, and more discreet in displaying his emotions than a Rispido.

Anybody who has anything to do with a Rispido will praise him right from the start for his equilibrium and keen judgment.

The Rispido moderates his own emotions and, what's more, establishes, through his sure presence, a degree of moderation. Despite the fact that he tries to remain inconspicuous, and keeps quiet unless asked something directly, a Rispido's opinion, though it may be terse, will be respected. He will give no more and no less than a factual account—painted in a few quick strokes with a humorous turn—then a diagnosis, and a projection, all very logical and rational, but with just the right dose of passion to be persuasive.

Everyone says that Rispidos are the very model of composure, charm, and prudence. Yet there is no one more obsessed with madness—secretly, agonizingly—than a Rispido.

A Rispido's equilibrium is as precarious as a tightrope walker's. No one knows it, but his rationality is the frayed rope on which he will lose his footing as he tries to keep the outbreak of his particular dementia from the others.

No madness is sadder than a Rispido's. He will go on reasoning at the level of the most lucid Aristotelian, and yet always have, latently, the anguished consciousness of his total, irreversible lunacy.

Regardless of their impressive logic, their unwavering temperance, Rispidos develop (secretly, agonizingly, like the entire process of their madness) several growing obsessions.

These obsessions begin as simple fears, momentary apprehensions, episodes that become more and more recurrent, till they turn into a form of insanity, if not a likely cause of death, as happens with a maniacal and demented fascination with the abyss.

Consequently, Rispidos cannot live on top floors. Their obsession with the void reaches the point that they believe they can exit a house via the balcony. Every Rispido who lives on a top floor ends up shattered down below. That's fate.

While sane, Rispidos spend their spare time playing games that use their intelligence. They like coming up with brilliant answers, playing football with two balls, 3-D chess, riding motorcycles blindfolded, and doing Chinese crossword puzzles.

But when they go mad, they play other games. For instance, their game of making brilliant answers becomes a tournament of savage irony, and they go so far as to remove the motorcyclist's blindfold, and blindfold the motorcycle itself.

KITREOS

Kitreos plan everything out before executing a task, before they take a single step.

Consequently, there are few occasions on which one observes a Kitreo taking a step. In general, they remain motionless, with a stern frown, clutching their chins with one hand. Kitreos think with their hands.

If a Kitreo doesn't think things through and dares to take a step, he will end up a complete fool, moving rhythmically through the sequence of steps he was going to take, and for this reason these stupid Kitreos are most useful for installing the movements of watches.

TROLUCHOS

The trouble with Troluchos is that each one is never to be found in the same quantity. On waking up, a Trolucho is singular: having just got up, he will look in the mirror, and sleepy-eyed, he will appear to be a single, complete individual with a head on his shoulders, with arms, with legs. He will smear on some shaving cream (Troluchos in this phase are used to shaving their entire bodies daily), and hold the razor to his cheek in the mirror, and lo and behold, he turns into two Troluchos. And if these two Troluchos take a long time to shave, each splits into two or three more Troluchos, until they can't all fit into the mirror anymore, and can't see themselves.

When a Trolucho needs to be in several places at a time in the course of a day, he can solve the problem simply by taking his time shaving.

As they are extremely sensitive, it is amazingly easy for Troluchos to become rapidly ill. The mere mention of a disease can actually infect them, just as to cure themselves they need only think of a remedy.

The Troluchos' physical sensitivity manifests itself in every way. You could say that their erogenous zones extend through their entire skins.

MODAR

The green land occupied by the Modar seems deserted. They cultivate portions of the land that seem uninhabited. The Modar aren't invisible, but there are no creatures more secretive. They walk on tiptoes, express themselves through mere glances and bland expressions, and are ignorant of music—if such a thing could be said in a land where all through the night, while the Modar are deep in sleep, springs of water fall from different heights and over various surfaces, producing recurrent, harmonious melodies, impelling clocks and wind-up toys that move to the water's pulse or emit wind-up music.

Among the Modar, doorknockers and bells are unknown. Nor are they familiar with bugles, bells, fifes, sirens or alarms.

Arguments literally have weight for the Modar. They can take any argument, grind it down to flour, and that way, as flour, they can weigh arguments peacefully. The Modar are very patient, it must be said, since it requires a great deal of patience to weigh out an argument. There are certainly some Modar who try to sneak a few interpretations into a ground-down argument—a hollow attempt at trickery. These interpretations are all smoke. A ground-down argument is a fact. Facts have weight.

So the Modar carry on discussions by weighing arguments in their highly esteemed scales, which are maintained by hand. There is a special phone they can use to call for a new pan or balance beam, and it will be sent in a hurry in an ambulance without a siren.

As an example, one side of an argument might turn out to weigh 3.5 kilos, and the other, 75 grams. In elections, everyone lays out their reasons for supporting a particular candidate; these reasons are ground down, and weighed out, and the candidate who has more tonnage of arguments on his side wins.

NOMIDOS

You can find some logic in anything. Nomidos say that if envy is wanting for oneself what another has, then actually having the other is the apotheosis of envy.

For Nomidos, envy is the most noble of sentiments, and one that facilitates their instinct to reproduce. In effect, when a Nomido desires another Nomido, his modesty forces him to clothe his lust in sentiment. So a Nomodio calls it "envy" when he experiences the noble sentiment to have another Nomido over all the other things he could possess.

When two Nomidos envy each other furiously, they give each other cameos, look for a place to go to bed—a task which takes almost a year, since they have to build the bed from scratch—and celebrate a solemn matrimonial rite in which they promise to envy each other with all their hearts (Nomidos have three hearts) for the rest of their lives.

LANICOS

Lanicos are good losers. They are such good losers that they have never won at anything. Because of this, one might say that Lanicos are the biggest losers in the world, and that as losers, they beat everyone.

Lanicos bet on the lottery and the races, on poker and roulette. They compete in every sport, including hog-stomping, Jello-straining and vase-chipping. They play and they bet and they always lose.

There is only one way a Lanico can't lose. It's if he plays or bets with another Lanico. In that case, there will be a tie.

Lanicos desire each other, have sexual relations, and reproduce only if they envy each other or hate each other. If two Lanicos love each other, you can be sure that they aren't Lanicos, because Lanicos don't know anything about love—they don't have any concept of it or instinct for it. Nor, in their language of grunts, is there so much as a phoneme to express this strange emotion.

Nevertheless, Lanicos are still brought together through the force of passions—hatred, greed, envy—that are every bit as irrational as love. Their coitus is more the result of rejection than desire. For Lanicos, sexuality consists of violent conflict, crises, alienation, anxiety, reciprocal beatings and manipulation, bantering and extreme contempt.

But there's one strange thing. Despite this near-apotheosis of spitefulness, the only time one Lanico thanks another—even as they're rolling on their backs, fighting with each other—is during the sexual act.

FEFOS

Fefos wear masks so that no one knows anybody else's face. Everyone gets mixed up because by law they change masks each day, getting a new one from inside a safe.

This ancient custom ensures that love lasts only one day, since if a Fefo falls in love with another Fefo, the next day he won't be able to tell which one it was.

VASINOCOS

Vasinocos never want roses. Vasinocos don't want anything. If a rose should turn up on a Vasinoco road, there would certainly be no one happier in the world than a Vasinoco to find such an exquisite delicacy, since it is known that Vasinocos consider a rose's thorn to be the most tempting and estimable little morsel.

PRADICOS

Pradicos keep track of time right down to the second. A Pradico King watches over all the clocks of his kingdom. Because of this, there has to be a day King and a night King, and only these Kings have access to the sacred Hall of Clocks.

Once, a long time ago, the night King had a little tiff with the day King over an hourglass, and playing a mean trick on him, delayed him for a few moments. In revenge, the day King swung back the pendulum— and so every day, each King changed the other's clock.

The dispute got to be so nasty that the Pradico people became aware of it. They promptly set all the clocks to the right time again, and locked up their Kings in the Northern Territories, where the Lacadonian descendants of both now live.

LACADONIANS

In Lacadonia, nobody knows what time it is. Or rather, everyone knows exactly what time of day or night it is, so nobody agrees about it. It's a hell of a problem for the running of trains.

The only thing they ever talk about it Lacadonia is the time.

YENYOS

Yenyos are binary. They function through the opposition of contraries. Their minds, however, don't reckon with contraries that number more than two. For Yenyos, then, things are either good or bad. Strangely, they never doubt that the opposite of good is bad.

Yenyos are like matched hinges in their crazy logic: opposite of "no" has to be "yes," and so on down the line; wakefulness, for instance, is the only alternative to sleep—which means that they don't see if their eyes are closed, and don't dream if their eyes are open.

Yenyo mental structure is basic and primitive: since it functions as a simple hinge, each wing of each hinge recognizes only its opposite. Though they are creatures of simple design, Yenyos nevertheless have a complicated mode of conduct, and one might even say that they are mixed up.

Yenyos are never what they seem: look down the street at a filthy Yenyo dressed in a crater-cleaner's overalls, covered with sulphurous mud, carrying in his hand the characteristic magnolia of that profession, and it turns out that such a Yenyo is a judge or a baker. One never knows if there is any sincerity in the way they act.

Yenyos suffer greatly from the contradictions of their intricate characters. Cyclical depressives, all Yenyos are in therapy.

Prisoners of dilemma, slaves of either the true or false, the good or the bad, the eternal or temporal, the spiritual or the corporeal, Yenyos, being simplistic, are compelled to act the way they think: they constantly stumble back and forth, wrecking their knees and whining, and each day going from hating their shrinks to loving them as one loves a friend who knows every secret.

Yenyos strip petals from daisies, have two rooms, see in two colors, love snow, and are swindlers.

Out of their characteristic melancholic states, Yenyos concoct a flabby, whining poetry that melts easily from their sticky, treacly hands.

Sometimes on Saturdays, Yenyos take advantage of the darkness to make fires in their fireplaces, and sit around in groups whining to each other.

Yenyo leaders are leaders for life; their principal responsibility is to guard the list of lies that they tell the other Yenyos in order to maintain their precarious system of government.

While half of all Yenyos are psychiatrists, a quarter of them are police. Moreover, a psychiatrist could perfectly well be a police spy.

A Yenyo experiences desire for a rose as negative, as the need for a rose, as anxiety for a rose, as a hole right in the middle of his soul where roses ought to be.

A Yenyo can buy up every rose in town in his search for the specific rose he wants and hasn't got, but he might just as easily start crying disconsolately, wondering whether he should become a rose grower, a rose seller, a rose thief—or just forget about the whole thing.

In general, every Yenyo ends up either giving up on these dilemmas, or going to a shrink.

WAXOS

Waxos are porous. The surrounding world fuses with them, seeps into them.

Waxos aren't familiar with most of the universe, but they are integrated into that part of it which is theirs, and this makes them happy.

Waxos have Moebius strips for brains: they know that there are no real contradictions, and that contradictions could only be possible in models of perception that deal incompletely with reality.

No one is friendlier than a Waxo. Or more amorous: they have a feline sensuality, which is consistent with the fact that their ideas are not distinct from their actions. They don't even have ideas as such, at least not in the sense that an idea is a representation, an image, a reflection of reality; Waxos are literally impregnated with their surroundings.

Waxos like garlicky foods, extremely red sunsets, piano music, and the play of the wind in the trees.

It's all the same to a Waxo.

All you have to do is give a Waxo a few good kicks, punish him for the slightest fault, and shout at him, if you want a Waxo to turn into a Yenyo. On the other hand, it is virtually impossible to turn a Yenyo into a Waxo.

Of all the species, not one matches the Waxos when it comes to poetry. All their thoughts (it's a crime to call them merely "thoughts") are part of a vast, free-flowing poem. But no one, not even Waxos themselves (who never bother to explain), knows what this endless canto says, because it never occurs to them to write anything down.

There's something else worth noting: Waxos have no language, nor do they need one, since proximity is all any Waxo needs to absorb the very substance, and the form, of other Waxos and their marvelous, singular poetry.

Thanks to their porous nature, and the Moebius-strip designs of their mental and glandular functions, Waxos do not recognize the quantitative. In spite of their clear perception of the simplest constituents of a given thing, they tend to see reality more as a kind of school of fish, or a constellation, as a totality in which each element participates harmoniously.

Waxo physiology makes it impossible for them to keep secrets, or have a private life. They haven't got the slightest desire to be in any way separate from other Waxos.

Moreover, internal evidence convinces them that they are not even individuals, but rather parts of a single great Waxo entity which itself belongs to a whole.

If a Waxo wants a rose, he undoubtedly believes that the whole universe is a rose, that *he* is a rose.

If a Waxo wants a rose, he doesn't see all the parts of the rose distinctly; for the Waxo, a rose is rose rapture, rose ecstasy, an endless, obvious metaphysical hallucination of roses.

ABOUT THE AUTHOR

Darío Jaramillo Agudelo was born in 1947 in Santa Rosa de Osos, Antioquia, Colombia. He is the author of several books of poetry, one of which won the Colombian National Poetry Prize in 1978, as well as a novel.

CPSIA information can be obtained at www.ICGtesting.com
Printed in the USA
BVOW041805251112

306414BV00001B/41/P

9 781934 851456